OF LOVE, LAUGHTER, AND EVERYTHING IN-BETWEEN..

By
Karishma Dasgupta

Printed in India

IndiePress

ISBN: 978-93-6045-835-5

First Printing, 2025

IndiePress

A division of Nasadiya Technologies Private Ltd.

Koramangala, Bengaluru

Karnataka-560029

http://indiepress.in/

Edited by Literary Connect

Typeset by MAP Systems, Bengaluru

Book Cover designed by Nikhil Kamath

Publishing Consultant: Souvik Bhattacharjee

To Nana –

Oh, how I miss you. Your presence still echoes in my heart, and I hope, in everything I do, I've made you proud and brought a smile to your face, wherever you may be.

To my sister, whose words of wisdom, when fear clouded my thoughts, echoed in my mind: 'What's the worst they can say? No, right? Then you have nothing to lose.'

To my mother, whose infinite patience I carry within me — a virtue that this book, long overdue, is a testament to.

To my father, whose strength and resilience I've inherited, shaping me in ways I'll forever be grateful for.

To my friends, whose unwavering support never faltered, regardless of their own struggles or the seemingly trivial nature of my concerns.

To my brothers: One who always listened to my woes, no matter how busy life became — proving that love isn't measured in time but in presence. The other who helped me realise the dream I once thought was impossible — becoming an author.

Author Bio

Karishma is a hopeless romantic with a knack for turning life's highs, lows, and "what just happened?" moments into stories that tug at your heart and make you smile. Inspired by love, heartbreak, and the relationships that shape us, Karishma writes with a voice that feels like a warm hug—or sometimes, a knowing nod over coffee.

A proud cat lover, Karishma carries the bittersweet memory of her beloved Cat, lost to love—a story as dramatic as it is unforgettable.

When not pouring her heart onto a page, she's likely at the beach, hypnotized by the rhythm of the waves, or off exploring a new destination, driven by an insatiable curiosity for life's wonders.

In Love, Laughter and Everything in Between, Karishma invites you to laugh, cry, and rediscover the magic in life's messy, beautiful moments. With stories that balance honesty and hope, this is a book that feels like a conversation with an old friend—one who knows just how to make you see the world a little differently.

Preface

Of Love, Laughter and Everything In-Between is a heartfelt collection of poetry that traverses the complex landscapes of love, loss, hope, and self-discovery. These verses offer an intimate look at the kaleidoscope of emotions that make us human—moments of joy, pain, resilience, and reflection.

The poems are not just words; they are windows into the soul of the author, capturing fleeting feelings and timeless truths. Each section of this anthology is carefully curated to guide readers on a journey through life's most poignant experiences, culminating in a celebration of hope, humor, and the little things that make life extraordinary.

Whether you are seeking solace, inspiration, or simply a moment to pause and reflect, this collection invites you to immerse yourself in its rhythm, its passion, and its honesty. Welcome to a world of raw emotion and poetic beauty.

Lucked Out

It was bright,

It was white,

Lo and behold, what a beautiful sight!

As calm as the lake,

Her face could not fake,

That's so much more than she could take.

Her eyes crinkled,

A smile drew up,

There was no space for doubt,

Or another meaningless sprout.

He was at the gate,

To decide her fate,

And the rest was history,

No time for bait.

He picked her in his arms,

Focused as a monk,

The bullet that stuck,

Had no space for luck.

She lay in his arms,

A smile still on,

If this is what love was,

She'd rather not be born.

Blind Love

Her hand moved slowly across his face,

Feeling every wrinkle and bump with her fingers,

He stood there silently, letting her express what was in her through her rapidly increasing breath and movement.

'You're wonderfully crafted,' slipped through her pursed lips,

Which she bit immediately.

His cheeks wrinkled further in embarrassment, astonishment, and at the audacity of her expression.

He lived in her heart, mind, body, and soul.

His breath moved through her, all through her bloodstream.

Who needs eyes when her world runs through her body?

Who needs eyes when, even with a blackout, her world is lit with the smile she feels on her fingertips?

Memories

Shrouded by memories of the past, she sat there, unwilling to believe,

Pressing her eyes shut as tight as she could, she sat there hoping to forget.

This couldn't happen again so soon, she soothed herself,

This shouldn't happen again so soon, she cried.

But there was no one to wipe her tears away,

No one to tell her that it was "okay".

What had she done wrong to deserve this?

What had she not done to deserve this?

Not an ounce of pity was seen,

Not a freckle of sadness was felt.

Is it like this when it's over?

Is it so cold and without a shiver?

Her heart bled, but still, she said,

Bless your soul, you heartless creature,

But may you never feel as deeply as me,

May you never see as blindly as me,

May your life not be as cruel as mine,

Open your heart, and may you be free,

To live a life as beautiful as it can be...

Hopes and Dreams

Every time I think of you,

There's a spark that flies, making me blue.

Truth be told, I live with you,

But far away,

And far from you.

Someday, I wish you would be near,

Closer to me,

Just by my ear.

Holding me,

And swinging me,

Never to leave me.

I know some dreams are lived afar,

I know some hopes are left ajar,

But this I hold close to me,

My heart be sealed,

Your love with me.

Illusions

Lay down with me and watch the stars in the sky,

Lay down with me and watch as the world passes by.

Fantasize, as I may, of the things that I say,

Living and reliving those dreams as I dream.

Laughing and feeling warm giggles inside me,

While warm tears slide out from my eyes to my cheeks.

Then I turn to look as you lay beside me,

But all I find is myself with me.

Tomorrow Maybe... Not

Dark, the world with shadows of fear,

Someone walks past and we cling to life so dear.

Be bold,

Be rebellious,

Be fearless,

Be brave,

For this life, we have for once to save.

A blink,

We miss,

And a decade is gone.

And gone so far,

Just memories remain.

Blind we are to the tomorrow we do not know,

Yet desperate we are to see what may not be.

Live by these rules if you'll take some from me,

Love,

Breathe,

Feel,

Just like your tomorrow will never be.

Through Thick or Thin

Sometimes she felt she loved too much,

Sometimes she felt she hoped too much,

Sometimes she felt she wanted too much.

Sometimes she felt she needed too much.

But love was all she ever learnt to give,

Hope was all she ever learnt to have.

Through tough times,

Through rough times,

Through inroads and out.

Love was all she needed to figure it out.

Repetition

She saw the face of despair once,

Never will she ever forget it.

She heard the sounds of silence, too,

Never will she ever forget it.

She saw the boat of hope sinking,

Never will she ever forget it.

Her eyes sparkled in memory of it all,

Never will she ever forget it.

And while she prayed never to see this war again,

History made sure she never forgot it,

And then it repeated.

Bare

Bare your soul to me, and I'll bare mine to you,

All your darkness, I'll take and give my light to you.

Bare your soul to me, and I'll bare mine to you,

All your sorrow, I'll take and give my joy to you.

Bare your soul to me, and I'll bare mine to you,

All your doubt, I'll take and give my faith to you.

Bare your soul to me, and I'll bare mine to you,

All your hurt, I'll take and give my love to you.

Bare your soul to me, and I'll bare mine to you,

All your pain, I'll take and give my pleasure to you.

Bare your soul to me, and still, I'll be there with you.

P.S. I Love You

P.S. I love you,

From the time I first saw you,

From the time I first felt you,

From then until now,

Time against time,

Every time I see you,

Every time I feel you,

Every time you're near me,

Every time you're with me,

Time holds still,

My life fulfilled,

Just you and me,

Forever to be.

P.S. I love you.

The Adventure Called LIFE

Come 2022, I thought I had my life all figured out — what I wanted to do, how I wanted to do it, where I wanted to be, and where I wanted to go. But, as they say, you can plan and plan however much you want, and life will surprise you with a plan of its own!

I surprised myself one day with a spontaneous trip, totally on an impulse, taking a little risk with the plans I had already set — taking life by the horns, as you may say, riding the bull for that adrenaline rush. 'One little detour, who cares?' I told myself. 'You only live once, lady. Bend the rules for yourself a little,' I pacified myself. Then, with a smile on my face and a sprint in my step, I packed my bags, finished a whole day at work — physically, at least (mentally, I was already on holiday) — and zoomed off to the airport to board that adventure plane I had detoured to a couple of months ago.

They say, 'When life throws lemons at you, make some lemonade.' Well, what do you do when life throws you into a FIELD of lemons and limes? No one tells you what to do then! How in the world do we navigate those odd, sour balls? Anyway, let's not detour anymore. Back to me, aboard the adventure plane, with that silly schoolgirl smile on my face, rainbows and clouds welcoming me, laying the pattern of a lifetime, luring me to the most beautiful pasture anyone could ever imagine. I sat there, sheepishly twinkle-eyed, waiting for that bumpy landing — believe me, smooth is never good.

While the actual landing at my destination was quite good, what awaited me outside the airport was a shocker, a surprise, and a whole lot of uncalled-for emotions. While I was looking forward to an experience, I found the reason behind those rainbows and clouds and everything else in between. As I said before, we can plan and plan, but life always has another plan in store for us. This life plan I had never dreamt of — well, at least not for the last two decades. Time flew by faster than the Hayabusa on my adventure, pushing and shoving me into places and emotions that had long left my soul or maybe ones that I had buried somewhere deep, never to be found again.

'NO!' I screamed to myself. 'You are not doing this again.' Sometimes, some things are better left in the ground. Digging them up is not going to do anyone any good, I pleaded. Tears ran down my already flushed cheeks as I tried to bring myself up. 'Ah, this is just adventure land. You'll wake up soon and smell the coffee.'

Well, let's just put this long story into conclusion and say, the coffee brewed, and it's still brewing — the aroma strong, just as I've always wanted. Sometimes, the plans we have for ourselves may just take an unexpected turn. Sometimes, you just have to let go. Sometimes, you just need to trust — maybe your gut, maybe God, or maybe the Universe, whichever one you believe in. Do I believe in fairytales? If you ask me, maybe I do. Maybe I'm living mine, or maybe I'm just making my regular day into the fairytale I've always wanted to live in. You can have whatever you set your mind to. Be it rainbows, fairies, or my favourite — LILIES!

Fact or Fiction

A walk by the sea,

A stroll in the park,

A fragrance flies by,

Like a spark in the dark.

It can't be,

It can't be true,

It's just a feeling,

And then I'm blue.

So fragile,

So intense,

So heavy,

So tough, I cannot carry.

Suddenly, I'm free,

Just like a bee,

Until I sting,

For peace to bring.

But then I fall,

Loud and hard,

Just like that dead tree,

That once stood tall,

But is now just hauled.

Set Free

My love,

I want to spend this lifetime and the next with you,

But only if you want to.

I love you beyond what you may imagine,

Even if you would try, you wouldn't fathom.

My love,

My life I have given you with glee,

But if you don't want it,

I'll let you be free.

For my love does not bind you to me,

But it's built to set you free.

Look through my eyes and you'll see what you mean to me,

But if it's too much,

I'll gladly let you be.

My love,

My life is for you,

But if you want to be set free,

I'll gladly let you be.

For my love is not binding,

It's meant to set you free.

A Prayer of Wishes

How many times I've wished I could hold you,

Hold you in sorrow,

Hold you in pain,

Hold you in stress,

And even in distress.

How many times I've wished I could hold you,

Hold you,

And caress you,

Calm your fears,

And wipe your tears.

How many times I've wished, and I've wished,

That someday,

Just one day,

My wishes be true.

But then, when I wish,

I wish you more strength,

More faith,

More love,

More life you can breathe.

And the more I wish, I wish you no sorrow,

No pain,

No sadness,

No tears that should rain.

Teach Me

Sometimes the hurt within my heart is so deep, I can feel it rip my life apart.

Sometimes the hurt within my soul is so strong, I can feel it tear me apart.

How can I begin to trust again, when all I can feel is this pain?

How can I begin to love again, when all I can feel is this hurt?

Oh, teach me how to love again.

Teach me how to trust.

Oh, teach me how to feel again.

Teach me how to live.

Down Below

My love, my love.

Where do I start?

What should I say?

Your wings are meant to fly,

Your words lead astray.

I meant to be the wind beneath those wings that fly,

To push you up,

To surge you through.

To let you live life, being just beside you.

You've taken off, soaring high above,

While I stayed beneath, far away from those wings below.

Don't look down now, for you may fall,

Beneath the earth,

Down through them all.

My love, my love,

I see you smile,

My heart for you,

My love all veiled.

Soar high, my love,

Reach for those skies,

But don't look down,

For you may fall,

Beneath the earth,

Down through them all.

A Dream So Real

Today, I dreamt about a dream so sweet,

My love was there,

Waiting for us to meet.

Oh, how I missed you,

It's been a while.

My life stood still,

My soul unfilled.

Where have you been?

I've missed you so,

My days all bleak,

My time so weak.

My dream so real,

I reached out to you,

You're shadow moved,

I watched you leave,

The loss I felt then,

Came back to me,

Your smile the brightest,

And yet, here I grieve.

Another Two

It's been a while since I've said, 'I love you.'

It's been a while since I've said, 'I miss you.'

Love, they say, is a mysterious thing,

Love, they say, is extraordinary.

I've felt it all,

I've seen it all.

My love for you, I'll do it all,

All over again,

Time and again,

Two decades later,

And add another four.

I told you I've always loved you,

I told you I'll always do.

I still hold true to what I said,

I'll still hold true for another decade or maybe two.

Empty

As time passes, they say I'd forget you,

As time passes, they say I'd let you go,

As time passes, they say I'd learn to unlove you.

How do I explain to them how I feel?

How do I explain to them who you are?

How do I explain to them what you mean to me?

Life moves on, they say,

Moves on to where I question?

Moves on how?

Moves on when?

'Don't love too hard,' they warned,

'Don't love too much,' they said,

'Don't love at all sometimes,' they cautioned.

But how do I tell them,

How do I tell them that I've waited for this day?

Waited for the day to love you,

Waited for the day to call you mine,

Waited for you all this time.

Fate

How do I tell you how much I love you?

How do I show you how much I care?

My love,

If ever there was a measure that could measure my love,

It'd break before the scale could fly like a dove.

I could write endlessly about my passions and love,

But nothing could compare to what's blessed from above.

My love, my love,

Don't believe those who tell you I've only loved you since yesterday,

For you've known my heart since I was barely a day.

At Least I Tried

Hop, skip, and jump,

Plop, I fell into it with a thump.

I smiled, I laughed, and I cried,

And it's okay,

At least I tried.

'Come to me,' I said,

'Let's spread our wings and fly,

Fly away with me,

Fly away without dread.'

How, what, why, when, where?

They didn't matter today, I said.

But you walked away,

And it's okay,

At least I tried.

Put your trust in me,

As I put mine in you,

Mine you shattered, but yours I'll keep.

We're not the same,

And it's okay,

At least I tried.

It's time to let go,

It's time to move on,

It's time to live and forget the life that's gone.

It was a dream,

I tried to live,

But now I'll mourn,

And it's okay,

At least I tried.

The Rat Race

How difficult it is nowadays to land a job. How even more tedious is it to find what you love? While a chance for a break came my way at the right time, unemployment is slowly creeping into my blood. We've all been taught to get onto this train before it leaves, and now, if we're not running, it's not normal.

While I sat longer on my sofa trying to figure out my next move, my next step, all I could do was stare at my laptop screen at all the jobs I wasn't qualified for. While I love writing and telling stories, I obviously wasn't 'qualified' for it, and studying to prove to someone to give me a chance was certainly going unnoticed.

Sometimes, when there's time on hand and the next appointment is a while away, I wonder, why do we have to run? Why aren't we taught to just walk to the next destination? Why are we always afraid that we will lose something if time is not met? As children, yes, we are told to study, but why do we all have to be the first in class to really matter? Just a thought: if we all get the first rank, then we're all the same, and if we're all the same, then what makes us different? If we're not different, then who are we really?

Fortunately, for some of you who do what you love, kudos to the one who believed in you. Salute. No, I'm not cursing or blaming anyone; I'm just reminiscing out loud, or rather in print. Coming back to the beginning of my topic, while being a writer is my dream, somehow, it's somewhere far away from where I am standing right now, and hopefully, it'll be closer soon.

As for the rat race, please stop running. There's no train to catch, and there's no trip you'll miss. The only trip you're missing is the one you're currently on — the present. So trust me, slow down, walk, breathe, relax, and enjoy the view.

Decades

She looked deep into his eyes,

Wondering if this was all.

He smiled back at her,

And took her to the fall.

She wiped the tear that slid off her face,

He promised he would change his ways.

She trusted again and held on tight,

He let go a little and built on the fright.

'Don't give up this time, as you said you won't,'

She cried and pleaded,

And prayed he'd moult.

'Come today, my love,

The day has changed,

Lovers till the end,

Soulmates forever,

Our story will be told,

For decades together.'

Time

Slowly, he crept up behind her,

Engulfing her soft, fragile body, he pulled her closer.

She sensed he had come,

But too weak to move,

She let him work his magic on her skin.

It was too late; their minds raced,

A tear, faster than their thoughts, rolled down their faces.

'Not now,' they cursed,

Brushing away that lonely one determined to show.

It was time, they were told,

Time for what, they reasoned.

Time had stood still for them since that awful day,

Time, they said, waited for none,

Time was there just to have some fun.

How ironic, they smirked.

Her back stuck to his chest today like a magnet.

'How romantic,' some would say,

How in love they still seemed, others would rhyme in.

But no one knew.

No one knew what was true,

Maybe everything was,

Or maybe nothing was.

Maybe this was a dream,

As real as it may seem,

Maybe it was just a dream.

Race With Me

Oh, how I love the smell of your hair,

The touch of your hand,

The mischief in your eyes,

Your breath on my skin.

Oh, how can I not fall in love with you,

Every single day, in every single way.

How brutal this world, that they won't let me love you,

How unfair this universe, that it won't let me be with you.

Someday, I tell you,

The universe will cry that it forced us to say goodbye.

But that day, it'll know,

Two stubborn hearts that refused to let go.

Soulmates

Today, I sat by my window, looking across at the sea,

And I found the soul that had been searching for me.

As we got closer,

With just the sea breeze between us,

We looked long and deep, with nothing to discuss.

It had taken us a while,

But now we were here,

Just him and me and nothing else to adhere to.

'Where have you been?' seemed to be a common thought,

For we had passed through hell and back,

Being nothing but distraught.

Stay now,

Don't let go, we sighed with a smile,

For who wants to stay without a soulmate, even if it's for a while.

One Drop At A Time

A drop fell to the ground,

A splatter I felt hard,

So I turned around,

And I saw red.

I saw black,

And I saw something more,

But, so scared, I ran ahead.

Another splatter then I felt,

This time harder,

This time stronger.

So I turned around again,

And I saw red,

And I saw black,

But I couldn't go ahead.

Too scared to move,

Too frozen to feel,

But I had started bleeding from my heel.

I watched it flow,

I watched it glow,

Slowly and steadily,

I watched it grow.

Growing and flowing,

Until I couldn't feel anymore.

I bled through a hole,

I bled through my soul.

One stroke at a time,

One strike at a time,

Until I couldn't feel,

Until I couldn't feel it anymore.

Mr and Mrs

Holding her hand tight, he led her ahead,

This place was special, like the moon that outled.

He'd kept it a secret from her for a while,

She was special, just like the twinkle in his eye.

The table was reserved,

The ambience was set,

Today, there was no chance for failure or regret.

He pulled a chair out,

For her to sit down,

Her face completely lit,

No chance for a frown.

Someone in the crowd pointed out twitching,

He ignored them,

He looked away,

And looked at her in awe,

She was bewitching.

They didn't matter,

He didn't care,

For to him,

Theirs was nothing but mindless chatter up in the air.

Sitting across from her,

He held her hand,

Firmly expressing,

With love in his eyes,

A smile on his lips,

Content on his face,

And pride in his glitch.

Until someone said,

'So sad about his Mrs,

She passed so soon,

Without his hugs or his kisses.'

Wounded

How would life be with just You and Me?

How would life be if not You and Me?

Thoughts run through my mind aimlessly,

Back and forth, back and forth so foolishly.

Sometimes, it's easier to forget,

Sometimes, it's easier to forgive,

But how can you forgive if you can't forget?

How can you forget if you can't forgive?

Everything unfair,

Everything unreasonable,

Everything so difficult for me to be gullible.

So easy you walk across, your legs in the air,

So easy you glide across, like you just don't care.

How foolish I feel,

I looked for a change,

The change in my face,

With the increase of your pace.

Fly away,

I pray,

For you to be blessed,

The wounds on my soul,

For me alone to be dressed.

My Soul

If I had a few days to live,

I'd pray to live them with you.

If I had a few days to breathe,

I'd pray to breathe them around you.

Take my life,

Take my breath,

Take everything,

Take me whole.

Leave me, but just a few moments,

To live and breathe around my soul.

The Lonely One

She walked on paths less trodden,

She swam across oceans less seen,

She dived into the skies wide open,

She breathed till her lungs burst wide.

Love, they told her,

Mocked her,

Threw pebbles,

Spat at her.

While no one saw her,

No one knew her,

No one even tried to feel her.

She walked,

She swam,

She dived,

And breathed.

And so she lived.

Vivid,

Happy,

And free.

Silence

She walked across the hallway with a tear rolling down her face,

He watched her in silence.

Opening the cupboard, she took out her clothes from the hangers,

He watched her in silence.

She packed her bag through her blurred vision,

He watched her in silence.

Dragging her bag heavily, she walked towards the door, stretching her hand to open it,

He watched her in silence.

She stopped,

Looking back at him one last time,

Her eyes could hold those tears no more,

They flowed like a stream across her already wet face, looking at him for an answer,

He watched her in silence.

She turned back, giving up,

One step in the air,

'Please don't go,' he muffled, falling hard to the ground,

'I'll die…'

The Wedding Story

Oh, the bliss of a wedding! Forgive me for loving the entire crazed fiasco around it, but I must say — guilty as charged! While I haven't been to very many of them, I've certainly watched, ogled, and drooled, starry-eyed at my screen, crying to bits every time a movie ends. The fact of someone finding love so pure stirs me into another world, another universe so far from our own — so true and wonderful that it makes me want to be there, breathing every second of their eternal love. Yes, I still believe in true love, in soulmates, in happily ever afters! Within this world of brutal cynicism lies my world of imagination and fairytales.

The day she decides he is the man she wants to marry is the day her world starts to tick afresh. A new day, a new life, a new tomorrow. As poetic and impossible as it may sound, don't we all shudder just looking at the bride while she takes those steps towards the altar to her future? That unsure smile, those glittery eyes, the tremble in her gait, the umpteen times she tries to swallow her jitters only to be met by the dryness in her mouth. And then you turn to her gaze, and you watch a mirror image — only this time, the image is stronger, but you can see through his eyes that he's melting faster than she is.

The romance turned into reality, and the realisation in that moment of truth that two lives are turning into one, two souls into one, and two dreams into one. And then they turn around as man and wife, hand in hand, step by step, breath by breath. I've always sat, looking at gorgeous couples smiling nervously at each other while their eyes twinkle the moment they catch each other's gaze. Yes, yes, I romanticise time, minutes, and seconds as well. How wonderful it is to watch them sweep the dance floor, joining everyone who took time to rejoice in their happiness. How deeply satisfying it is to dance with the bride and groom, who take time to notice that you've come to share their joy.

I've been a tad bit unlucky to be unable to participate in some of my most beloved's happy moments, but never have I been away in thought. While the rest that I've caught, trust me to be that awe-struck, forever open-mouthed relative! While I will continue to watch and cry at every happy ending story, may the ones who've had their happy endings bless us all with more.

Twisted Time

Softly, he caressed her cheeks,

Singing sweet nothings in her ears.

Gently, he tucked her hair,

And let all her goosebumps bare.

Her smile spread across her face,

His smirk held onto her gaze.

She turned pink,

He turned red,

But not a word either said.

And then, as time stood still,

They prayed for one last will,

To keep the past,

To let it last,

And then, one moment,

One was gone,

And one stood holding on to that one last song.

No Boundaries

She flew like a bird through the hurdles,

Nothing seemed to stop her,

Not the heat, not the sweat, not the threats.

One down,

Two down,

Three down.

She then swam across easily through her next pent-up hurdle,

'She's a breeze,' they cheered together like a firmly fixed girdle.

Then just as she touched the finish line,

She turned to her side and smiled,

Eyes all eager, sparkling, and bright.

Somewhere in the crowd,

He smiled back,

The same animation twisting the ring on his finger he held tight.

Hers

She fell in love again,

This time, he seemed different.

But fear leapt in her soul every time he was sweet.

Fright engulfed her every time with his tweet.

He seemed genuine,

But she had seen a lot.

He said he wanted to be with her forever,

But she had her doubts.

Refuting her fears and inhibitions,

She believed him.

Refuting all the negativity in her,

She let him move forward.

She let him enter her soul,

She let him enter her being,

She let him be one with her,

She let him be hers.

Broken

Promises are meant to be broken, they told her,

But her foolish heart said, 'No.'

They're all the same, they warned her,

But her foolish mind said, 'No.'

Don't let them in this time, they pleaded with her,

But her foolish soul refused to let go.

She said, 'Yes,'

She said, 'Yes,'

And then she sat in a complete mess.

Unaware,

Spent,

Alone.

Bridges

I walked alone for days,

I walked alone for months,

I walked alone for years,

Building walls more than bridges.

Then, one day, you came along,

Building bridges to those walls.

Betrayal

Oh, so bitter, you cursed soul,

Why didn't you vanish with the one who created you?

Why do you still live here amongst us to kill us?

I thought you'd left me alone that night,

When I walked away from my love, my life,

But no, you chose to stay on like a shadow,

Lurking and prowling behind me!

Why, oh why, when I trust, you know?

How? Oh, how? Oh, tell me, how do you know?

You blow me, you kill me, and then try to soothe me,

Wiping my back, feeling my scars, when they're given by you,

And then you smirk and give me some more.

Songs and Melodies

He walked through the door, ripping open the strings of my heart,

Not knowing the pain of heartbreak, I smiled, letting him invade my soul.

Naive and innocent, I hugged him, my soul ecstatic,

While he smirked at my ignorance,

I blushed at it with joy.

My fate unknown to me,

My life still unscarred,

He began to write his melody.

While I still sing his songs with joy,

He goes on to write new rhapsodies.

The Tick in My Head

There's a click in my head that goes tick-tick,

And no matter how hard I try, I just can't flick it.

I whine, and I cry, and I try to break it,

But that bloody tick-tick will just not take it.

I try to run, and I try to hide and hope I find a place where I can keep it,

But it seems like it's there and seems everywhere,

That bloody tick-tick, I believe, has some flair!

It clutches and holds and sucks onto my blood,

This bloody tick that's stuck like a flood.

I wait, and I watch, and I wonder what it is,

And that's when I hear another tick-tick.

Damn you, tick-tick, where do you come from?

And then I remember it's a slumber I need to get up from!

When You Love Someone

Love is silent,

Love is slow,

Love is something someone may never know.

Love so hard,

Love so true,

Love someone like you would love you.

Never hurt,

Never push,

Never fight a bleeding bush.

Love so true that they would miss you,

Love someone like you would love you.

Immovable

She slept under covers all night,

All day, she didn't move.

She watched the world move by morning and night,

But not a muscle in her body moved right.

Someone knocked,

Another one called,

Another one tried more than just haul.

She heard it all,

She watched it all,

But not a muscle in her body rocked at all.

She lay there still — on her bed,

Lay as though she was already dead,

Lay there watching the world move by,

But not a muscle in her body let her touch her sky.

For the Sheer Love of Sunglasses

Yes, I love sunglasses. Size doesn't matter in this case, let me tell you. I love them all — big, small, medium, coloured, discoloured, or whatever the case may be! It's not really ironic when you think about it, considering my work involves revolving around these fascinating objects of self-pleasure. Now, let's calm down on those thoughts, and let me control some of my adjectives, if not all or many. Let me tell you how I first fell in love with this piece of perfect human creation. Well, I still don't have a baby, or else that'd be the second-most perfect creation! Yes, my weird sense of humour is still very much alive!

Step into 1980-something, and I see this gorgeous woman walking across my hallway, wearing literally the biggest piece of eyewear I could've possibly seen, and lo and behold, it was love at first sight! Well, yes to both of your thoughts, but let's stick to the subject matter, shall we? And in case you're still wondering, that was my grandmother strolling into my home on a visit. I still remember her oversized square-shaped sunnies covering almost half of her face, but oh, with what poise she'd carry them off. Come to think of it, we'd probably not be able to pull that off even today. Yes, I adore her, and yes, I've eyed those bloody squares for more than a decade! Yes, I've mustered up my courage to pick two of those overwhelming babies for myself, but they still lie in my drawer in hopes of seeing the light of day!

Sunglasses are my absolute favourite. They can light up my day like no man ever could! I have a drawer full of them, and I couldn't care less! My most favourite, and I think I'd have a lot of supporters for this one, are reflectors! Be it blue, pink, green, grey, you name it! I love them! I feel they let me breathe, stay alive, and rejuvenate! I'm addicted to them, lucky me I can ogle at them all night and day! Trust me, you can never go wrong with them! Okay, jokes aside now, while summer's gone in some places and others have yet to experience it, it's time to bring out all those hidden beauties and have some fun, shall we? But then again, who needs a season or an occasion to love these beauties!

Walk of Fire

How many more scars until it'll stop bleeding?

How many more wounds until it'll stop hurting?

How many more days until I stop counting?

How many more times until I stop feeling?

I've seen these steep roads,

I've walked these crooked paths,

I've passed some unclaimed roads,

I've felt some miles apart.

Funny how words are never enough,

Funny how time is never enough,

Funny how feelings get so tough,

Funny how thoughts get so rough.

Spare me, O heavenly one,

Don't let me see what's already begun.

I've walked the walk of fire once,

Don't take me there for another chance.

You Killed Me

I lay here, 6 feet under, cold and numb,

I lay here, 6 feet under, with bruises on my waist and thumb.

If you could see, you would know,

The pain I felt even while I looked at me from somewhere you couldn't see.

The love we had was for people to see,

But deep down, somewhere inside, you killed me.

I smiled and grinned every time someone asked me your name,

But deep down inside, I knew you already killed me.

Today, when the bruises are visible, and my body is cold,

You lay there comfortably in your blanket, hoping no one will ask, 'How come these look old?'

I cried and screamed every time you laid your hand on me,

I yelped and screeched every time you swung that leg on me.

My friends pretended they couldn't hear me,

My family pretended they could feel me,

But no one, no one, just once came to rescue me.

My pain was mine,

My hurt was mine,

Mine alone.

And now, when there's nothing they or anyone else can do,

They continue to pretend,

To love me,

To rescue me,

To know me.

When I'm Gone

Will you miss me as I miss you?

Will you shed that tear as I shed for you?

Will you look at my pictures and think of me as I think of you?

Will you miss my hand as I miss yours?

Will you miss my kisses as I miss yours?

Will you miss my laughter as I miss yours?

Will you miss my smile as I miss yours?

Will you miss me as I'll miss you when I'm gone?

Remember

Remember the time you let me be who I was?

Remember the time you let me cry without judgement?

Remember the time you didn't ask me why?

Remember the time you accepted my craziness?

Remember the time you calmed my anger?

Remember the time you understood my incompleteness?

Remember the time you accepted me for just who I am?

I could list down a million memories and a zillion reasons why,

But for you,

Remember only,

From all these molehills,

Grew something for you,

From admiration to love to life.

Invisible Strings

I realised how short life is today,

I realised how much love I still had to display.

I realised that no matter how much we try,

There will always be something that's missed.

I realised that some promises may be broken,

And you may regret those forever.

I realised that sometimes a smile is just a facade,

And we all assume that it's not.

I realised how much I really love you,

And how much I wish I could tell you.

I realised how many years have passed without you calling my name,

And how much I wish I could hear you.

I always knew that my heart was with you,

But I only realised those strings were true,

When you went down under and pulled those with you.

Live a Little

There are strings that tie you down,

Nails that pin you down,

Ropes that don't let go,

But you have to break free.

Break free from what weighs you down,

Break free from what pulls you down,

Break free if it's not meant to be,

Break free from you and me.

No one said we were meant to last,

No one said you cannot erase the past,

Let go,

Breathe,

Live.

My Cup of Love

I love slowly,

I love soft,

And then suddenly,

I fall hard.

Hold me tight,

Don't let me go,

For I don't know how I'll love again, so.

I emptied my cup,

Till my last drop fell,

I thought I was done,

But then I heard your voice,

And it strung that bell.

That familiar sound,

That familiar face,

And slowly and steadily,

My empty cup is filled.

Those years that went by,

Those wounds that I healed,

Those times that I promised myself,

Not another tear for the ones that I sealed.

You came chasing in,

Your lips with a smile,

My heart you stole again,

Not even for a while.

My empty cup,

You filled again,

Until the last drop,

You'll savour it again.

My Fairytale

Hold my hand when I'm not looking,

Pull me closer when I'm least expecting.

Love me like I've never been loved before,

Feel me to my soul like it's never been done before.

It's the fairytale love that I've always dreamt about,

It's the fairytale love that I've always lived without.

Is it so difficult, I wonder, to be loved?

Is it so difficult, I wonder, to be true?

Walk with me and try to see what I see,

Walk with me and try to see how I'm free.

Love is just a feeling so easy to flow,

So much to learn from and so much to grow.

My Blue Blue Sky

I looked up at the blue sky today and wondered why the sky was so blue.

I looked up at the blank canvas and wondered what I could draw.

I looked up at the shades of blue and couldn't help but wonder about you.

You make me think about you,

You make me love you,

You make me miss you,

But, oh man,

You do make me so blue, too!

My many words,

My many feelings,

My many moments captured between me and you.

How do I keep myself from falling for you,

Even though I know there's this life,

And it's just me and you.

The Next Five Years

I asked my love one day,

'Where do you see us in the next five years?'

He replied to me, quick to say,

'Not five, but six, I'll tell you,

There'll be cake, and there'll be me,

I'll be cutting it, and I'll be free.

For five, I'll tell you what will be,

There'll be you, and there'll be me,

For this is God's plan,

For you and me.

We met for a reason,

The reason he knows,

He brought us together,

And a miracle arose.

You are my miracle,

The miracle I'm grateful for,

For this life was different,

Before you came,

And now it's different with colours and games.

I let go of you once,

A folly of a child,

I'm not letting go of you again,

No matter sun or rain.'

I looked at him with love,

With tears in my eyes.

My man, my love,

I loved you as a child,

I loved you while you were wild,

I loved you in silence,

And I loved you with pride.

And now I get to love you,

And everyone gets to see,

But no one can ever fathom how much you mean to me.

Turkey - With All Puns Intended, I Ate None!

Why, hello there! Yes, my very weird sense of humour overflows onto paper, too.

If you haven't figured it out yet, like all small-budget trips, I too began my travel journey through Turkey. Keeping this brief to read and relish, but still a little inquisitive to ask me more — *yalla*!

Being on a 15-day solo trip, I must tell you that everyone associated with me thought I was totally bonkers when I decided to backpack through Turkey. This was completely unknown territory, all on my own, and considering the very recent situation at the very airport I had to land at — it was a challenge to my sales profession! Fortunately for me, I was on my way to the airport while they frantically paced in their respective homes, trying to pull me out of my cab and back to 'safe' shores!

Considering I'm telling you about the awesomeness of my trip right now, you are right, even though I do apologise, I have no gifts to offer apart from some more stories and the miracle about me being alive — I did make it out of there — very alive, in all terms of the word — ALIVE!

Yes, travelling alone is a challenge. I won't tell you that it was all hunky-dory or anything along those lines. As a matter of fact, it did get lonely some days. But most days, it was enriching, fulfilling, and free! I must've walked miles and miles in search of new places, famous milestones, and anything that put a sticker on my map, but mind you, I found none! If, of all the things I did there or learnt or understood or starved for, I learnt to be grateful. How often we take for granted all the things we have, not once being grateful for thanking the one who blesses us.

I couch-surfed, walked alone, explored deserted byways, and did the wackiest of things I'd never thought I'd do, but somehow, I'm back here telling you about my adventure. I can't wait to take another trip, explore another country, find another opportunity to speak in sign language, or in my case, starve myself from food but fill my soul with complete happiness and gratitude!

Just Me and You

Walk with me on this winding road,

Walk with me till the end.

Walk with me through thick and thin,

Walk with me like a friend.

Hold my hand and guide me through,

Hold my hand, and don't let go.

Hold my hand, and we'll find a road,

Hold my hand, and we'll glide it through.

Worry less about "what if",

Worry less about "but how",

Worry less about "because",

Worry less about "let's try,"

It's time for us to make this through,

It's time for us to be me and you.

Let's walk this path less trodden,

With stones and thorns and bones and horns.

Let's walk it through like I said before,

Let's walk it through, just me and you.

A Bid of Value

Reminiscing today, I wondered why I feel the way I do.

Sometimes it makes sense, and sometimes I try to make it try to.

I love hard,

I love deep,

I love like you've never seen love before.

How do I make sense of this kind of insanity,

Like the love I felt for you within me.

Where do I start?

Where do I stop?

Where do I draw that line in between?

You broke me once,

You broke me twice,

You broke me every time you tried to seem so wise.

I read those words between those lines,

I cried myself to sleep so many times,

Your cold touch,

Your cold heart,

Your icy breath all over my soul.

How do I forget those words you said?

How do I move on from those times I bled?

Life is hard,

Life is tough,

Life is rough,

But it still goes on.

I swore I'd never love again,

At least not someone like you, I won't,

Those icy hands,

That hollow soul.

Those empty hopes,

And empty words,

The life with you gone down the hole.

I'm glad I left when I did,

Never again to see you, I bid!

Tales of My Love

Today, as we shared tales of love,

Tales of light and tales of aspirations,

Tales of fondness and tales of affection,

I saw that glimpse of hope and happiness,

In your eyes, too,

The same I see in my eyes for you.

Oh, tell me please,

You love me more than I love you,

That you'll cross those seas for me and you.

My shores I leave behind,

In hopes of calmer seas and silent rivers,

Oh, tell me, love, you'll take my hand and guide me through.

Oh, tell me, please,

You love me more than I love you,

That you'll see my dreams through like they've come from you.

My trust, my love, I put in you,

My hopes and dreams all pass through you,

My love, my love knows no bounds when it comes to you,

My heart, my soul, all belong to you.

Gonna Love You Forever

She sat there watching the love of her life hum a tune.

She sat there watching as he smiled and swayed, blowing away like a dune.

She sat there watching the curves around his mouth break into a smile.

He sang of love and life and heartbreak.

He sang of rain and sun and snow and wind.

She watched in awe, amazed that someone like him could exist.

She watched in awe, marvelling that she could breathe the same air as him.

She watched in awe of him.

A tear slid down the side of her cheek, warming her already flushed face.

And then she watched him some more.

She watched him till she tore.

And then she watched him some more...

I Get to Love You

Today, I heard something that brought tears to my eyes.

Today, I learnt something that made my heart skip a beat.

Today, I saw something that took my breath away.

It's not every day that I get to feel what I felt today.

It's not every day that I get to live how I live today.

It's not every day that I get to be how I am today.

It's not every day that I get to tell you how much I love you from just two feet away.

But what I do get,

Is,

I get to feel,

I get to live,

I get to be,

I get to love you,

Every single day,

And that I wouldn't change for anything else,

Anytime or anywhere.

I get to love you.

Every,

Single,

Day.

The Arms of My Beloved

Do you know every time I want to tell you I love you, I pen a poem down?

Do you know every time I miss you, I pen a poem down?

Do you feel how I feel when you're not around me?

Do you feel how I feel when you're not here with me?

Oh, how my heart bleeds when I can see you but cannot touch you.

Oh, how my soul wails when I can hear you but cannot feel you.

Counting the days, the minutes, and the seconds seems like second nature to me.

Reliving the moments and memories seems like living a dream to me.

Be patient, my love, I pacify myself.

A few more moments and you'll be where you're meant to be.

Within the arms of your beloved,

Hidden where no one else will be.

A Million Lifetimes

Within this heart lies a million secrets,

Within this heart lies a million reasons.

I go back and forth with the reasons why,

I go back and forth with the reasons why not.

How long must I wait for you? I wonder sometimes,

But how long is long enough, I wonder at others.

I told you I'd wait a million lifetimes for you,

And I'll tell you again that plan is true.

Infinity is not enough to love you, my love,

So I'll wait another few to say I've loved you through.

Since 2002

Sometimes I wonder,

Why is it that I love you so much?

Why is it that I can never tire of telling you?

Why is it that through all of it, it still doesn't feel like it's enough?

Why do I sometimes have the urge to just call you and tell you I love you?

Do you feel the way I do?

Do you feel like you love me too?

Do you feel the emptiness in your soul like I do without you?

Do you cry that lonely tear when you don't find me near, too?

How do I explain to you the love that's there within me?

How do I explain to you the years that I've spent without you?

How do I explain to you those sleepless nights I've had since 2002?

How do I explain my overflowing heart to you?

Come hold my hand, and you'll feel my heartbeat.

Hold me closer, and you'll feel the rhythm sheet.

Hold me closer and let our hearts sync.

Hold me closer, and let me not think.

Hold me tighter and let me pass on to another life,

For this one being yours and yet so far away from you hurts me more than it did in 2002.

The Secret of Happiness

In shadows and dark places,

I look for solace and solitude.

In chaos and noise,

I look for peace and sanctity.

In bright lights and sunshine,

I look for calmness and stability.

And in failure and letdowns,

I look for success and happiness.

Reminiscing

Through the morning catch-ups,

And midday updates,

Evening teas,

And nighttime routines.

Through the sleepy good nights,

And muffled 'I love you's,'

I love you more,

I love you still,

I loved you then,

And I always will.

Where To Go. How To Go. Go? No?

There we go. The plan is to go on a vacation, but where and how to go is still the question! Looking back on my "Vacation Plans", it always takes me back to 2012.

It was this bright early Sunday morning, a couple of friends and me: a 'couple' includes 13 other people apart from me. Yeah, I know, 13 being the very odd, maybe superstitious number I should've known better. But sometimes, you just want to be a little positive!

So there we were, all screaming and shouting with a headcount like we were on the way for a picnic, hoping no one would lose their way to the door or car standing right outside. Somehow, we managed. Defying all odds against a friend's best friend, I jumped right into the front seat of his car like there was a rocket someone lit in the wrong place on my anatomy, but nonetheless, I won! As you must know now, yes, I love winning! Even if it was as small as a 25 fil chocolate you'd offer me, I must win! :D

Reaching our destination — which was a nearby mall for an early morning breakfast — we grabbed the largest table we could find, added another large table, and began the most difficult part: ordering breakfast! Once that beast was tackled, we decided to move on to the next most important bullet of our very important hangover, forgetting the early morning meetup.

Looking at the two people who proposed the super awesome Europe Tour, 24 dreamy eyes looked hungrily at them, partly reminiscing about the hangover and partly, no doubt, for the sheer excitement of the trip! Strangely, they realised through some heroic male sensing hormone in their progesterone-puffed-up bodies that we poor little hungry children needed some fodder for our dreams. Taking it on as a responsibility to help the underprivileged, they began to dissect the plan in their heads when, at that very second, we heard: 'Scrambled eggs with sausage,' 'Sunny side up with toast,' and before the third order could come up, we realised that our hungover bodies responded better to food counts than a lecture, no matter how interesting the professor or the topic of discussion may be!

Our tired, hungry ears and crying stomachs seemed to grab the food right out of the kitchen, and before we knew it, the food was a far better topic of discussion than our impending flight details out of the desert to the land of green. With the supply of an unlimited variety of food — imagine 14 hungry stomachs, 14 different levels of hunger, along with the 14 different capacities and, of course, 14 different just an extra side, it won't be too much - TRUST ME!

The transition from 'We take a flight from Dubai to London' to 'Could you please pass me the ketchup' to 'Guys, I think we should try Thailand and Bangkok' to 'I think Turkey is gorgeous' to 'I don't know what else was totally mind-boggling!' Our poor little waiters trying to figure out if we were really going to travel somewhere, eat our breakfasts, or try to fetch them more food was indeed a sight to watch for the sober!

After gorging almost half their kitchen, I believe, we travelled half the world right in our seats, reached back to the same place where we began, paid our bills, thanked our servers, patted our overfull bellies, and walked out like bosses, still rich in our pockets with joy and money, and a verbal acknowledgement of the 8-odd grand we may end up spending shopping and travelling in half the countries we mentioned while we fueled our empty tums!

Now, four years later, the vacation is still pending, the belly is still filling, and the money is the only one I see travelling! Yikes!! Ka-Ching!

My All

I stood at the shore that day,

Wind blowing in my hair,

My breath shaking,

My body trembling,

Memories flooding,

My heart filling,

My head spinning.

I stood by the shore that day,

My life flashing before my eyes,

My feet letting go of the ground,

My tears escaping the borders of my lids,

My skin burning,

My flesh melting.

Oh, how I missed your warm breath on my face,

Your touch,

Your hands,

Your body,

Your soul.

Oh, how I'd give anything to be by your side again,

My life,

My soul,

My all.

To My Love

For anyone who has a doubt about my love for you,

Tell them I've loved you since the day I first saw you.

For anyone who doesn't believe my love for you,

Tell them I've loved you since the day I first touched you.

For anyone who thinks I don't love you,

Tell them I've loved you since the day I first felt what love was.

And for anyone who still can't fathom my love for you,

Tell them I've loved you even though I thought I lost you.

I'll Always Choose You

If today we're far away and you're not sure if I'm here to stay,

Remember, I'll always choose you, no matter the distance or the day.

If tomorrow our paths go awry and you're not sure if I'll still be there,

Remember, I'll always choose you, no matter what or where.

And if someday you feel maybe I won't choose you after we're old and frayed,

Remember, I'll always choose you,

No matter if we're young, old, blue, or grey.

My Silver Lining

And then one day,

You slid into my life,

Like a breath of fresh air,

Like a taste of adventure,

Like a mystery unsolved,

Like a missing piece of a puzzle,

Like a silver lining on my cloud.

My One and Only

As I lay by your bank,

With nothing more but Him to thank,

I wonder how I've lived so far,

Alone with me,

My life ajar,

And then I see,

My life and me,

So whole with you,

So alone without,

And that's why I say,

When it's time to rest,

Into your breast, I'd like to lay,

For that one last dance,

That one last act,

With you alone,

I'd like to play.

Companionship

Last night, I prayed for peace,

For calm,

For love,

And companionship.

Then I closed my eyes and rested for a bit.

The next day,

I found peace,

Calm,

And love,

But no companionship.

So I asked again.

And I found peace, calm, and love,

But no companionship.

So I asked again.

'Do you not hear me?

Am I not your child?

Can't you see me begging for companionship?'

Then I looked up,

Tears welling up in my eyes,

Lips trembling in plea,

Trying to understand the signs.

But once again,

I found peace, calm, and love,

But all of that I found within me.

And then, I learnt what the signs were telling me.I

was worthy of me,

I was to be my own companion,

Before I found the one who is meant for me.

Little Things

I always say,

Sometimes, we meet the right person at the wrong time,

And the wrong person at the right time.

But what if the time is always wrong?

What if we're supposed to break it,

But we're not really that strong.

You came into my life like a gentle breeze,

With the setting sun and a little tease.

Saying the right things,

And doing the right things.

Saying all the things I wanted to hear,

Doing all the things I imagined to see.

And here I am now.

Why do I feel for you like I do?

Why do I crave for you like I do?

Why does it feel so good to speak to you?

Why does it feel so empty without you?

Are words, thoughts, and feelings better left unsaid?

Are they better left understood?

Or is it just another way not to be misunderstood?

Thoughts

Sometimes, I wish I could speak my mind,

Sometimes, I wish I could be more kind.

How I wish it were easier to say,

The words that I want,

The words that I may.

Life is short, some say,

Life is long, the others dismay.

I live by the day,

The moment,

The time.

I live with what will be mine, is mine,

Maybe not today,

But some other time.

What If I Am Wrong?

There's that light I see at the end of my road,

A light so bright and strong.

I walk towards it like I know where I'm going,

But what if I am wrong?

The ups and downs,

The curves and straights,

I think I know them all,

So,

I walk with trust, resolve, and faith,

But what if I am wrong?

These roads so sharp,

These curves so steep,

I feel like I will fall,

But I trust and walk,

Not one to talk,

But what if I am wrong?

I've left my home,

My love,

My life,

To follow that light so bright,

So,

I trust and walk,

Not one to talk,

But what if I am wrong?

The Transition

I once loved a boy so much it was beautiful,

We kissed over the skyline,

We kissed under the moon,

We kissed while it was day,

And also by noon.

We loved so hard,

We loved so strong,

We loved like there was no tomorrow,

Like there was no wrong.

And then one day,

As we grew older,

When girls became women,

And boys became men,

He chose to stay a boy,

While I became a woman.

Virtual Reality

With the number of dating websites and virtual profiles we swap between our daily lives, somehow, I feel we have forgotten to live the real deal. How often I catch myself staring into my phone, smiling away, or laughing at a joke that only my phone and I find absolutely hilarious — it's unbelievable!

Is this really what we are progressing to? Is this really the life we dreamt of and waited to live when we were asked to study at our tables? VirtualMe.com! Jeez!

But on the other hand, introverts like me (if I'm really allowed to call myself that) really dig into it sometimes! Like, for example, over the numerous and countless times I've stared into my computer and phone, I've realised midnight chats are mostly with our neighbours (again, if you get my point), not that I mind, I've come across some really wonderful neighbours, and about the rest, let's not get into that. More often than not, I always wonder, where do these nice night owls really go during the day? I've constantly bumped into the most hideous ones during regular daytime hours.

Coming back to my midnight hour, my safest and most active hour of my life, I'm usually browsing through my pending jobs, YouTube, Facebook, Google — you name it! The other time, there was an update about this app called 'Whisper' on Facebook. Quite intrigued by its name, I scrambled for my phone, punched in my app store, and off I went in search of this so-called secret platform.

I must say, I was a little sceptical about the app, but it did, and still does, work absolutely fine — until you realise the "Tinder" mania runs in there, too. And then, like one big hot potato, I fell flat to the ground. Like, damn, what's with Tinder and people? I know it's nice and all, especially the swapping and the "It's a match!" popping up in green right into your face like it's your phone telling you, "Yes, it's time you had a life, I'm just so tired of you — I too need some alone time!"

But please, at least try to get to know me before wanting to jump undercovers with me!! And that's how Whisper came, and Whisper went, just like how it's supposed to be in reality — a "Whisper", soft, least troublesome, and quiet!

So, while I chatted with some really nice souls there and, of course, ignored and blocked the rest of them, I really missed the reality of friendships, or should I say, the beginning of friendships. The awkward smiles, the introductions, the eye-reading, the facial expressions, the laughs together when you speak at once, or when you realise you both love the same things or find out that you have a friend in common! Wow! I want all of that, each and every bit of it, I do!

Virtual reality is so unreal and artificial, and it's not what I'm looking for. This is now another mission I write to myself: I need to get out there and make new friends, enjoy a sunset, have a cup of coffee, and who knows, I may meet someone just like me — another archaeologist of reality.

My Whole

My love,

My heart,

My soul,

Every time I'm not with you,

My heart feels like it's missing a piece.

My heart races,

My breath shortens,

My body lacks its regular rhythm.

'How could you love someone so much?'

I'm asked oh so often,

But, my love,

How could I tell them what you mean to me?

How could I tell them what I feel for you?

How could I tell them how my life is with you?

How could I explain to them how my life is without you?

You, my love,

Are my life,

My heart,

My soul,

My all.

Without you,

My life is far, far away from being whole.

Crazy But True

Every time I look at you,

I see something you won't find true.

Your eyes,

Your nose,

Your lips,

And even your fingertips.

They make me spin,

They make me fly,

They make me drown,

And I don't know why.

You call me crazy,

You say I'm mad,

But my love,

My only love,

Believe that this is the best life I've ever had.

Lovers Lie

'You're the most beautiful woman I've ever seen. Every time I look at you, my heart skips a beat,' he confessed.

Caressing her face, he drew her closer and kissed her deeply. Tears slid through her eyes in silence.

Then he held her face in his hands and looked at her with those eyes she'd always seen — loving, caring, admiring.

He then kissed her forehead with a promise to always love her, no matter what swirled her in a dance till she giggled like a schoolgirl, and then left to go to work.

As she watched him leave the building, still smiling from her giggles, she felt her heart begin to get heavy from realisation.

She walked to the mirror, trying to look into it with confidence but still looking at her feet, head down. Slowly, she began to move her head and then her eyes to her reflection — she collapsed, falling to the ground hard.

Acid did that to the skin — she had melted that day. Her world had melted with her. She felt no hope, no love, nothing. She turned stone.

But, what she had forgotten was him. Her strength then, her strength now. He hadn't changed, though she felt she had — for the worse, but he stayed the same. He never failed to tell her how much he loved her. He loved her soul, he would say, and he sure did prove it every single day.

Because of him, she was coming back, coming back to human again, accepting again, breaking sometimes, but still living. She lived for him — as he lived for her.

She loved him.

Come Back

My mind races back to when I called you to say that I was home,

After all these years,

I was finally home.

I hadn't seen you in so long.

I had to speak to you,

I had to call you,

There was so much to talk about,

I was all grown up now,

I missed you.

I still remember dialling your number and waiting for you to answer,

'Hello, Gorgeous,' I chuckled over the phone as soon as you answered,

I was so excited.

In a second, you knew who I was.

Your voice still resounds in my ears,

'I'll see you then,' you smiled over the phone after promises of our meeting.

Promises are meant to be broken, they always say,

But I refuse to accept it.

I still feel like it's a dream,

I still feel like I'll hear about you,

I still feel like you'll answer if I call you.

You have to answer.

But I'm so scared to try,

I'm scared I'll be disappointed,

I know I'll not find what I'm looking for anymore,

No matter how hard I try.

Please come back.

You have to come back.

You can't just leave like that without a bye.

Shadows in the Dark

It's been dark for a while now,

But shadows I can see.

Trying to adjust somehow in this dark,

Using a technique I read online,

But nothing seems to work.

I hear sounds,

I hear friends,

I see people all around.

Someone came in.

Someone walked out.

Someone said something.

Someone had a doubt.

I listened,

I heard,

I helped,

And smiled,

And then again,

I blacked out.

Of Love and Hurt

I close my eyes,

I try to sleep,

But the memories of you,

Are left too deep.

How do I try?

Why should I try?

I try to reason,

But then I'm left to dry.

I'll tell you this,

Don't love too deep,

Don't love too strong,

I'll plead to you,

For I'm not wrong.

It'll rip your heart,

It'll tear apart,

It'll bleed you dry,

It'll make you cry.

The tears will heat,

Your cheeks will burn,

Your heart will ache,

Not much it'll take.

But then you'll learn,

And then you'll live,

You'll learn to love,

And more to give...

Believe

She always believed in love,

Always believed love conquered all.

She always believed in love,

Always believed that, that was all.

She always believed in love,

Always believed even through each fall.

She always believed in love,

Always believed in heart,

Always believed in them,

Until they tore her apart.

Spare Me

Softly, she cried, her pillow soaking wet,

No one would know her deepest, most silent regret.

She calmed her mind,

Her body,

And her soul,

Until she could feel no meaning of being whole.

She prayed while she cried,

Those tears burning up her cheeks,

Burning until she could feel those cheeks no more.

'Spare me,' she pleaded to the one who heard her,

'Spare me from this torture and pain,

Spare me,' she pleaded, having only peace to gain,

Even though she continued to cry in vain.

My Eyes

Look through my eyes, and you will see,

What you really mean to me.

Sometimes I'll say it,

Sometimes I won't,

But never will I say I don't.

Don't ask me what,

Just stop, see and feel,

The sparkle I see in you,

Is what makes me real.

Through Our Years

After all these years,

My heart still races every time I think of you.

It still skips every time I see you.

It still flutters every time I touch you.

It still melts every time I feel you.

And after all eternity,

I still want to feel the same.

Magnets For Life

Life is absolutely blissful when you have friends around you. And if you have a crazy bunch like mine – God bless you, too! I've never been able to calm down about them or around them; I somehow always feel like I'm unable to justify their awesomeness — be it in print or in heart! Of course, all parts of them being so awesome is because they have me, but eh!

I have come to realise that people, no matter where they come from, what they do or did, or what they want to achieve, at any given point in time, all anyone ever wants is to be happy, content, and satisfied. All of us are literally the same like we were all born from the same embryo and popped out of the same womb. Think about it, aren't we all magnets? Sticking to everything that we are attracted to and just letting something unappealing to us slip off? To be honest, for me, I don't have just ONE magnet! I have a whole bunch of them — held on to them for the sheer life of me. Living memories, reliving them, laughing at their stupidity, and even discussing the stupidity to laugh all over again! Yes — this is us, or should I say, this is ME.

One particular memory I have is of one of my bestest (yes, loving this word as much as I love her!), oldest, and closest friends ever. We were in second grade then, yes again, we've been friends since then. This was right after some kind of an outing we had. As we sat there waiting for our respective parents to come along and pick us up, this friend of mine decided to munch on a candy much larger than her 2mm mouth! So, off she went, meticulously unwrapping the candy and popping my favourite flavour into her mouth while I looked on wide-eyed as she savoured the best with her oh-so-tiny taste buds without a care in the world of being called fat or any other term we later begin to learn as humiliation or contempt.

Greed slipping all through her bloodstream, she attempted to swallow the whole 2-inch candy in a single bite, instantly choking on the very pleasure of her greed. I vaguely remember her face turning pale and yellow and her gasping for breath while my teacher looked on casually, asking me to give her a hard smack on her back in order to jerk that damned candy out of her system. Of course, no matter how old or young you are, friendships have unspoken rules of never causing harm to another, right? So, keeping the rule in mind, I patted her back like she was doing an excellent job of getting choked and turning pale, and had a wonderful dramatic touch to it. I mean, so what if she didn't share her candy with me? She was my friend, and I patted her away!

So, while she choked and I patted and my teacher laughed in sheer amusement, the entire class just sat there in silence, like watching an opera of the damned candy that choked my friend. Nonetheless, my teacher finally got off her chair, and mind you, she was quite a woman — in all aspects if you ask me — walked over to us and delivered the loudest thud I've ever heard on my poor friend's back! Lo and behold — pop came the sacred candy too scared for its own life, I assumed!

My much-relieved friend shrieked in the joy of being very alive, right in time to embrace her very confused mother, who entered the classroom to claps and a standing ovation!

Since that day, until today, that pale candy eater has been my magnet through thick and thin, filtering through my torture and still surviving our almost 26 years of awesome friendship. And, of course, much to the amusement of her mother, who still can't believe what holds us together — the very weird girl who stood red-faced right next to her very yellow-faced daughter, who looked like she'd just taken a good spanking from me for not sharing some candy!

Of All The Reasons

Of all the reasons I could list down for why I love you,

The most I'd tell you,

Is because,

Only you know the extent of my insanity and still have the courage to love me, too...

You Before Me

You before me,

Always been for me.

You before me,

Always meant to be.

You before me,

In all that words can be.

You before me,

In all my life to be.

Only in death should it be,

Me before you...

As for everything else,

You before me,

Always has,

Always is,

Always will be,

You before me...

War

Saying good night, she let out a silent sigh, and that lonely tear left her eye,

War was difficult,

But her country was more precious,

So she sacrificed her babies,

Sacrificed her life,

And shed that blood for her countrymen...

War was difficult...

One Step Ahead... One Step Behind...

As I walk alone down this long, winding road, I begin to wonder,

I begin to wonder, when was the last time I wandered out alone without a thought of you or a memory in mind?

Taking one step forward with one foot ahead and the other one behind,

I realise you are still with me, tugging there strongly on that foot behind.

I have walked and walked, leaving you behind, but some part of me you have taken with you.

Therefore, I realise that maybe I don't need to erase you from my mind,

Maybe I don't need to forget you.

Maybe I just need to accept,

Accept that you will always remain with me,

Accept that no matter where I go or what I do, that part of me will always remain with you,

Always with you, one step ahead and one step behind.

Picture This

Imagine walking in a tunnel with just a faint light to lead,

Now the lights are out, but you're yet to be freed.

It's darkness,

It's uncertainty,

It's confusion,

And panic.

There's anxiety,

There's fear.

There's stress,

And distress.

I live through this,

I breathe through this,

I walk alone even through this.

Picture me a soulful song,

Picture me a picture so strong,

I dream of living a life stress-free,

I dream of living just being me...

Silent Killer

Nothing can kill me, I tell you,

Nothing at all.

I've seen far too much, to be honest.

I'd say I'd do very well under pressure,

Under stress,

Under torture,

Under pain,

Under defeat,

Under strain,

But silence...

This one...

Damn!

This one just kills me...

Home

Sometimes, I walk through the day,

Knowing not where to stay,

And then, out of the blue,

Someone just walks me through,

And when I turn to see,

It's you with me,

Right there,

Right then,

Side by side,

Hand in hand,

Promise to keep,

Promise to hold,

Until we're old,

Your heart — my gold,

My soul, you hold,

And then, you know,

Like they always say,

My home I've reached,

In your arms each day...

Lost

Shake me a little,

I seem to be lost.

Wake me a little,

I'm sure it won't cost.

My heart cries for thee,

My soul yearns in blood.

Where have you gone?

Why can't I see?

Why can't I see,

What I have done to me...

The Death of Me

Close your eyes and look at me,

Feel me with your breath...

Touch me with your memories,

Until I reach my death...

Miming

Every time I see you smile,

My heart will skip,

I'll shed a cry.

I say I love you,

A million times,

And I'll say it again,

With a million mimes.

You are perfect,

Just as you are,

You are the best,

Let go of the rest.

You have it within you,

You always had,

You must remember,

And never forget...

Marry Me No... Yes? Please? Maybe?

Being an Indian girl from a semi-conservative family is a little tough, if I may say so from experience. So when it came to the big 'M,' something needed to be done—and it needed to be done ASAP—I needed to HIDE!

Boy hunting, son-in-law hunting, grandson-in-law hunting, nephew-in-law hunting.... all the possible in-law hunting scenarios were happening around my home lately, and it was getting too hot to handle for me any longer. Something needed to be done NOW, like—RIGHT NOW!

It's funny how, when I'd give 'how to evade a marriage conversation' advice to a friend, it was much easier than taking that bloody advice for myself! I felt like I needed to get six feet under most of the time. Unless I was working, then I was fine, because I had money, and money made me happy. And being happy meant I could shop, and when I shop, I'm happy.... and I can shop some more! Then, it's just a vicious cycle.... and then let's just let go of the shopping—it's rent month next month, I need to save.

Coming back to my impending marriage, here I was, outwardly all calm and serene, trying to be the best at my job, trying to be the best daughter my parents could have so that they'd get a little jealous and refuse to give me away to some stranger they thought would be best suited for me and my tantrums, and realise that they had to keep me entirely for themselves. But no, my parents, I must also realise, are Indian parents—the most perfect, the most responsible, and not forgetting, the best—so no jealousy!

As though me running around like I had a mad cow chasing me wasn't enough, one day, out of the blue, there was a friend request on LinkedIn (of all the places!). And before I knew who it was, my phone rang with my father on the other line, screaming, 'I like this boy, I like the father, now see if you like him!'

Cut. So there I was, staring at my screen, not knowing what just happened, wondering if I was seriously going to marry the boy smiling back at me through a Polaroid picture or if I was just going to lose my mind!

My head began to swirl, my skin began to twirl, and the pit in my stomach fell flat to the ground. I was done for! There was no escape! The boy impressed my father, the boy's father impressed my father— me? I'm not impressed by anybody! And certainly not at the smiling 32 teeth I could see!

Moving on, somehow containing my anxiety and completely frazzled brain, I went ahead and spoke to Mr. Smiles. Well, he was sweet to speak to, and I believe honest, but something inside me was jumping up and down, making me feel all queasy and not so happy. This lasted for a few days, considering Indian arranged marriages worked like that—where you had to speak, then accept and then make babies ASAP! Not good!

Turns out, that sweetness was quite sticky, oozing out of him like sweat oozed out of my body post a gym session with my super-hot— only until he didn't reach the numeral value of 7 on a set—trainer (another interesting story)! He was very sticky indeed.

After a few calls here and there, I politely declined his advances towards marriage, probably breaking his heart considering the ridiculous amounts of status updates and love forwards I received from him. I had to. He—though not intending this badly at all—was like that painfully sweet sugar syrup you greedily gobble up right after having the most heavenly tasting, melt-in-the-mouth, warm, moist, soft, yummy, mind-blowing gulab jamun, hoping it will leave a worthwhile leftover taste of heaven in your already sweetened mouth. But then.... all hell breaks loose!

It's never worth it—the very sweet syrup that you gulped so hungrily and courageously leaves you with such a weird bittersweet aftertaste that you're not sure if you should gulp down water to ease yourself or suffer the brunt of your greed and let your beloved gulab jamun happily float in your stomach acids with a little syrup of its own! Yes—that was him.

Therefore, bye-bye, my very sweet but not for me acquaintance. I hope you've found your own gulab jamun and are making her float in your sweetness!

So far, I have managed to suppress my parents' eagerness towards my marriage. Let's see how long this works for... Until then... See ya later, alligator!

Insanity and Beyond

Remember me in your silence,

In your chaos,

In your incompleteness,

In your doubt,

In your confusion,

In your detest,

In your anger,

In your hatred,

In your defeat,

Remember me.

But most of all,

Remember me in your insanity...

Hopes

When I say I love you,

I don't expect you to say it back,

I just hope that you do, too...

When I say I miss you,

I don't expect you to say it back,

I just hope that you do, too...

And when I lay my heart out for you,

I don't expect you to lay it out, too,

I just hope that you would see it through...

Found

Smirking, he looked at her and said,

'Looks like you have loved and lost.'

Smiling, she replied,

'I have loved and therefore found it all...'

Untied

Her beauty didn't lie in the beauty of her eyes,

But in the soul that she wrapped up,

And let him untie...

Until Then

If I told you how much I love you,

It'd be a metaphor.

If I told you metaphors,

It'd be a lie.

If I lied to you,

I'd rather die.

Maybe in death, you will know,

So until then...

Free

Breathing in the country,

She spread her arms wide open,

The purest of smells raced through her nostrils, her lungs,

She felt them revive her, release her.

She felt purified.

Sadness,

Deceit,

Defeat,

Loneliness,

Everything out.

Out like the black smoke after a put-out fire.

Black smoke,

That's what she harboured.

Now she was free,

Free again.

From clutches,

From chains,

From herself...

Tug of War

Have you ever been in a tug of war between your soul and your brain?

The feeling of the existence of every cell in your body screaming out for no reason at all?

The chaos in your mind and soul debating between calm and cluster?

The unfortunate mismatch and match of every fear and mania?

The loss of words to explain or pacify?

A state of complete reclusion and disdain?

Have you?

Have you?

I have...

The tug of war between my soul and brain...

Loving You

Loving you, they said, was wrong,

Loving you, they said, was impossible,

Loving you, they said, was the worst that I could do,

Loving you, they said, was not supposed to happen,

Loving you, they said, was not just about me and you...

But you tell me,

What's worse,

Loving you or never knowing love at all?

Little Lessons

You ask me about my best lessons learnt,

I'll show you my heart.

Do you see those lines in white?

Those are the scars that healed.

Now, do you see the ones in red?

Those are the ones that are fresh.

Do you see the ones that bleed?

Those are the ones that never fill.

Now, do you see the smile on my face?

That's what my story says,

Little lessons here,

Little lessons there,

Bigger reasons everywhere.

Did I learn from hurt?

Or did my heart just become a yurt?

Every scar,

Every trench within my heart,

Reveals a story,

A lesson learnt,

A heart that still believes,

Even though it is burnt...

The Realisation

Yes, well, I know, this is a very vague header to start with, but what can I say, it was indeed a realisation!

I have been writing poetry, short stories and other—in serious terms—forms of literature since a very early age. I still remember, I think, I was in the 7th grade when I handed out a poem I'd written to my best friend, who indeed still holds the same title until today! Yes, we pride ourselves on our tolerance of each other, or rather, she prides herself on her tolerance of me. Wait, she's too lovely to pride anything, and that's why she still holds her position strongly! Yes, I blabber, it's a childhood problem I'm really not into fixing—it keeps you hooked on reading, wondering where I'll stop, right? I probably won't.

Anyway, let's get moving onto my realisation of a talent I thought I had and decided not to pursue, but instead, get into some fast-tracked career and goal-driven path that I probably wasn't. Well, I had goals, and I made a career, but certainly not in the field I should've loved or wanted, but instead in a substitute—a substitute. Like all hot-blooded youngsters, I rushed into applying for colleges and catching trains to meet potential deadlines, never realising I was actually giving up on a dream—my dream!

Fast forward 14 years—from graduating to finishing a fulfilling decade of my career based on my education, I still felt there was a void I couldn't fill anymore. Something was missing. Something amiss.

While I didn't do any injustice to my chosen career or the people who chose me to represent them in the world, I was doing great injustice to myself—told you I loved poetry! Yes, of course, I had a blog going parallel to my work, but I wasn't able to give 100% to either. Try doing two things simultaneously; something will always get a 1% deviation.

While I'm not the kind of person who likes an attention crunch, and work is no longer a pleasure like it used to be, I had to make a decision. A decision that was expensive—not just the money, but my time. I do value my time as money, anyone's time as money. If someone offered to have a cup of tea with you, you had better value it. If you weren't that important, they'd rather be plopped somewhere else enjoying a margarita, maybe!

See, I told you I wouldn't stop! But now I think it's time, time for me to move on, time for me to stop, stop running, stop fighting, stop compromising. This was the day of my independence, the day the earth stood still—oh wait, that's a movie—but hey, that's the best explanation in just six words!!

The Beginning...

IndiePress

The best route your story can take.

To publish your own book, contact us.

We publish poetry collections, short story collections,
novellas and novels.

contact@http://indiepress.in/

Instagram- indie_press

Made in the USA
Columbia, SC
23 June 2025

59784955R00143